Manifestation JOURNAL

This Book Belongs To :

MY VISION BOARD

MANIFESTATION

Date: / /

Today I Want To Manifest:

Today I'm Grateful For:

Visualization:

I am...	
I feel...	
I have...	

My Daily Affirmations:

1.	
2.	
3.	

Actions To Take:

1.

2.

3.

TRACKING & REFLECTION

Slept From :....... To : ......

☐ Good Dreams ☐ Bad Dreams ☐ I don't Remember

Notes :

GOOD HABITS TRACKING :

think POSITIVE

- Cups Of Water I Drank Today : ....
- Exercises : .... Time : ....

☐ Meditation ☐ Reading ☐ Take Vitamins ☐ No Sugar

☐ Eat Healthy ☐ Drink More Water ☐ Socialize

☐ Be Positive ☐ Pray ☐ Family Time ☐ Sleep Early

MOOD TRACKING :

Happy ☐ Sad ☐ Anxious ☐ Lazy ☐ Sick ☐ Flirty ☐ Inlove ☐ Angry ☐

Notes :

Your Daily Dose Of Affirmations :

I am intelligent

I am strong

I am happy

I am blessed

I am compassion

I am a great person

I am a positive person

I define my individuality

I have decided to stick with love

I accept joy

I accept abundance

I accept honesty

I accept a healthy relationship with everyone

I accept a healthy body

I accept a healthy mind

I accept myself for who I am

PROMPTS

Do you control your thoughts or do your thoughts control you?

MANIFESTATION

Date: / /

Today I Want To Manifest:

Today I'm Grateful For:

Visualization:

I am...	
I feel...	
I have...	

My Daily Affirmations:

1.	
2.	
3.	

Actions To Take:

1.
2.
3.

TRACKING & REFLECTION

Slept From :....... To : ......

☐ Good Dreams ☐ Bad Dreams ☐ I don't Remember

Notes :

GOOD HABITS TRACKING :

think POSITIVE

- Cups Of Water I Drank Today : ....
- Exercises : .... Time : ....

☐ Meditation ☐ Reading ☐ Take Vitamins ☐ No Sugar

☐ Eat Healthy ☐ Drink More Water ☐ Socialize

☐ Be Positive ☐ Pray ☐ Family Time ☐ Sleep Early

MOOD TRACKING :

Happy	Sad	Anxious	Lazy	Sick	Flirty	Inlove	Angry
☐	☐	☐	☐	☐	☐	☐	☐

Notes :

Your Daily Dose Of Affirmations :

I am filled with joy

I am filled with happiness

I give and receive love

I am the hero of my own story

I work hard to achieve my goal

I am a good person

I believe in myself

I am filled with love for myself

My body is a gift and I love it

My mistakes are stepping stones for success

I am worth everything I desire

I have everything that I desire

I am worthy of love

People love me for who I am

Everybody respects me

Everyone loves me

PROMPTS

How can you cultivate more joy in your everyday life?

MANIFESTATION

Date : / /

Today I Want To Manifest :

Today I'm Grateful For :

Visualization :

I am...	
I feel...	
I have...	

My Daily Affirmations :

1.	
2.	
3.	

Actions To Take :

1. ______

2. ______

3. ______

MANIFESTATION

Date: / /

Today I Want To Manifest:

Today I'm Grateful For:

Visualization:

I am...	
I feel...	
I have...	

My Daily Affirmations:

1.	
2.	
3.	

Actions To Take:

1.

2.

3.

TRACKING & REFLECTION

Slept From :....... To : ......

☐ Good Dreams ☐ Bad Dreams ☐ I don't Remember

Notes :

GOOD HABITS TRACKING :

think POSITIVE

- Cups Of Water I Drank Today : ....
- Exercises : .... Time : ....

☐ Meditation ☐ Reading ☐ Take Vitamins ☐ No Sugar

☐ Eat Healthy ☐ Drink More Water ☐ Socialize

☐ Be Positive ☐ Pray ☐ Family Time ☐ Sleep Early

MOOD TRACKING :

Happy	Sad	Anxious	Lazy	Sick	Flirty	Inlove	Angry
☐	☐	☐	☐	☐	☐	☐	☐

Notes :

Your Daily Dose Of Affirmations :

I deserve to be loved

I am beautiful

My black skin is beautiful

People are fond of my skin

People are attracted to me instantly

My skin glows

Every part of me is beautiful

I am comfortable with my own skin

I have a strong willpower

I am proud of myself

I am proud of my culture

I am proud of my upbringing

People around me are supportive

People around me encourage me

PROMPTS

What impact do you want to have on the world?

MANIFESTATION

Date: / /

Today I Want To Manifest:

Today I'm Grateful For:

Visualization:

I am...	
I feel...	
I have...	

My Daily Affirmations:

1.	
2.	
3.	

Actions To Take:

1.

2.

3.

TRACKING & REFLECTION

Slept From :....... To : ......

☐ Good Dreams ☐ Bad Dreams ☐ I don't Remember

Notes :

GOOD HABITS TRACKING :

think POSITIVE

- Cups Of Water I Drank Today : ....
- Exercises : .... Time : ....

☐ Meditation ☐ Reading ☐ Take Vitamins ☐ No Sugar

☐ Eat Healthy ☐ Drink More Water ☐ Socialize

☐ Be Positive ☐ Pray ☐ Family Time ☐ Sleep Early

MOOD TRACKING :

Happy	Sad	Anxious	Lazy	Sick	Flirty	Inlove	Angry
☐	☐	☐	☐	☐	☐	☐	☐

Notes :

Your Daily Dose Of Affirmations :

I am focused

I am disciplined

I am courageous

I am fearless

I inhale confidence and exhale doubts

I am a magnet of success

I am better than I was yesterday

I have a vision and I work for it

I am bigger than my circumstances

I am bigger than social pressure

I am successful and everyone knows it

I am a product of peace and righteousness

PROMPTS

What sort of energy do you give out to others?

MANIFESTATION

Date: / /

Today I Want To Manifest:

Today I'm Grateful For:

Visualization:

I am...	
I feel...	
I have...	

My Daily Affirmations:

1.	
2.	
3.	

Actions To Take:

1.

2.

3.

TRACKING & REFLECTION

Slept From :....... To : ......

☐ Good Dreams ☐ Bad Dreams ☐ I don't Remember

Notes :

GOOD HABITS TRACKING :

think POSITIVE

- Cups Of Water I Drank Today : ....
- Exercises : .... Time : ....

☐ Meditation ☐ Reading ☐ Take Vitamins ☐ No Sugar

☐ Eat Healthy ☐ Drink More Water ☐ Socialize

☐ Be Positive ☐ Pray ☐ Family Time ☐ Sleep Early

MOOD TRACKING :

Happy	Sad	Anxious	Lazy	Sick	Flirty	Inlove	Angry
☐	☐	☐	☐	☐	☐	☐	☐

Notes :

Your Daily Dose Of Affirmations :

I am a strong black man who deserves all the good things in life

Things that make me different are things that make me ME.

I am grateful for everything the universe has blessed me with

I respect everything and everyone in my life

My love and positivity brings me joy and happiness

Thank you universe for everything.

PROMPTS

Describe your dream life.

MANIFESTATION

Date: / /

Today I Want To Manifest:

Today I'm Grateful For:

Visualization:

I am...	
I feel...	
I have...	

My Daily Affirmations:

1.	
2.	
3.	

Actions To Take:

1. ____

2. ____

3. ____

TRACKING & REFLECTION

Slept From :....... To : ......

☐ Good Dreams ☐ Bad Dreams ☐ I don't Remember

Notes :

GOOD HABITS TRACKING :

think POSITIVE

- Cups Of Water I Drank Today : ....
- Exercises : .... Time : ....

☐ Meditation ☐ Reading ☐ Take Vitamins ☐ No Sugar

☐ Eat Healthy ☐ Drink More Water ☐ Socialize

☐ Be Positive ☐ Pray ☐ Family Time ☐ Sleep Early

MOOD TRACKING :

Happy	Sad	Anxious	Lazy	Sick	Flirty	Inlove	Angry
☐	☐	☐	☐	☐	☐	☐	☐

Notes :

PROMPTS

How would you feel if your desire manifested?

MANIFESTATION

Date : / /

Today I Want To Manifest :

Today I'm Grateful For :

Visualization :

I am...	
I feel...	
I have...	

My Daily Affirmations :

1.	
2.	
3.	

Actions To Take :

1.

2.

3.

TRACKING & REFLECTION

Slept From :....... To : ......

☐ Good Dreams ☐ Bad Dreams ☐ I don't Remember

Notes :

GOOD HABITS TRACKING :

think POSITIVE

- Cups Of Water I Drank Today : ....
- Exercises : .... Time : ....

☐ Meditation ☐ Reading ☐ Take Vitamins ☐ No Sugar

☐ Eat Healthy ☐ Drink More Water ☐ Socialize

☐ Be Positive ☐ Pray ☐ Family Time ☐ Sleep Early

MOOD TRACKING :

Happy ☐ Sad ☐ Anxious ☐ Lazy ☐ Sick ☐ Flirty ☐ Inlove ☐ Angry ☐

Notes :

PROMPTS

How do you feel when you see a sign from the Universe?

MANIFESTATION

Date : / /

Today I Want To Manifest :

Today I'm Grateful For :

Visualization :

I am...	
I feel...	
I have...	

My Daily Affirmations :

1.	
2.	
3.	

Actions To Take :

1.

2.

3.

TRACKING & REFLECTION

Slept From :....... To : ......

☐ Good Dreams ☐ Bad Dreams ☐ I don't Remember

Notes :

GOOD HABITS TRACKING :

think POSITIVE

- Cups Of Water I Drank Today : ....
- Exercises : .... Time : ....

☐ Meditation ☐ Reading ☐ Take Vitamins ☐ No Sugar

☐ Eat Healthy ☐ Drink More Water ☐ Socialize

☐ Be Positive ☐ Pray ☐ Family Time ☐ Sleep Early

MOOD TRACKING :

Happy	Sad	Anxious	Lazy	Sick	Flirty	Inlove	Angry
☐	☐	☐	☐	☐	☐	☐	☐

Notes :

PROMPTS

What's stopping you from going after your dreams?

MANIFESTATION

Date : / /

Today I Want To Manifest :

Today I'm Grateful For :

Visualization :

I am...	
I feel...	
I have...	

My Daily Affirmations :

1.	
2.	
3.	

Actions To Take :

1.

2.

3.

TRACKING & REFLECTION

Slept From :....... To : ......

☐ Good Dreams ☐ Bad Dreams ☐ I don't Remember

Notes :

GOOD HABITS TRACKING :

think POSITIVE

- Cups Of Water I Drank Today : ....
- Exercises : .... Time : ....

☐ Meditation ☐ Reading ☐ Take Vitamins ☐ No Sugar

☐ Eat Healthy ☐ Drink More Water ☐ Socialize

☐ Be Positive ☐ Pray ☐ Family Time ☐ Sleep Early

MOOD TRACKING :

Happy	Sad	Anxious	Lazy	Sick	Flirty	Inlove	Angry
☐	☐	☐	☐	☐	☐	☐	☐

Notes :

PROMPTS

What is your goal for the year?

MANIFESTATION

Date : / /

Today I Want To Manifest :

Today I'm Grateful For :

Visualization :

I am...	
I feel...	
I have...	

My Daily Affirmations :

1.	
2.	
3.	

Actions To Take :

1.

2.

3.

TRACKING & REFLECTION

Slept From :....... To : ......

☐ Good Dreams ☐ Bad Dreams ☐ I don't Remember

Notes :

GOOD HABITS TRACKING :

think POSITIVE

- Cups Of Water I Drank Today : ....
- Exercises : .... Time : ....

☐ Meditation ☐ Reading ☐ Take Vitamins ☐ No Sugar

☐ Eat Healthy ☐ Drink More Water ☐ Socialize

☐ Be Positive ☐ Pray ☐ Family Time ☐ Sleep Early

MOOD TRACKING :

Happy	Sad	Anxious	Lazy	Sick	Flirty	Inlove	Angry
☐	☐	☐	☐	☐	☐	☐	☐

Notes :

PROMPTS

What is the purpose of money?

MANIFESTATION

Date: / /

Today I Want To Manifest:

Today I'm Grateful For:

Visualization:

I am...	
I feel...	
I have...	

My Daily Affirmations:

1.	
2.	
3.	

Actions To Take:

1.

2.

3.

TRACKING & REFLECTION

Slept From :....... To : ......

☐ Good Dreams ☐ Bad Dreams ☐ I don't Remember

Notes :

GOOD HABITS TRACKING :

think POSITIVE

- Cups Of Water I Drank Today : ....
- Exercises : .... Time : ....

☐ Meditation ☐ Reading ☐ Take Vitamins ☐ No Sugar

☐ Eat Healthy ☐ Drink More Water ☐ Socialize

☐ Be Positive ☐ Pray ☐ Family Time ☐ Sleep Early

MOOD TRACKING :

Happy	Sad	Anxious	Lazy	Sick	Flirty	Inlove	Angry
☐	☐	☐	☐	☐	☐	☐	☐

Notes :

PROMPTS

I know I will succeed because…

MANIFESTATION

Date: / /

Today I Want To Manifest:

Today I'm Grateful For:

Visualization:

I am...	
I feel...	
I have...	

My Daily Affirmations:

1.	
2.	
3.	

Actions To Take:

1. ______
2. ______
3. ______

TRACKING & REFLECTION

Slept From :....... To : ......

☐ Good Dreams ☐ Bad Dreams ☐ I don't Remember

Notes :

GOOD HABITS TRACKING :

think POSITIVE

- Cups Of Water I Drank Today : ....
- Exercises : .... Time : ....

☐ Meditation ☐ Reading ☐ Take Vitamins ☐ No Sugar

☐ Eat Healthy ☐ Drink More Water ☐ Socialize

☐ Be Positive ☐ Pray ☐ Family Time ☐ Sleep Early

MOOD TRACKING :

Happy	Sad	Anxious	Lazy	Sick	Flirty	Inlove	Angry
☐	☐	☐	☐	☐	☐	☐	☐

Notes :

PROMPTS

What emotions do you need to let go of in life?

MANIFESTATION

Date: / /

Today I Want To Manifest:

Today I'm Grateful For:

Visualization:

I am...	
I feel...	
I have...	

My Daily Affirmations:

1.	
2.	
3.	

Actions To Take:

1.

2.

3.

TRACKING & REFLECTION

Slept From :....... To : ......

☐ Good Dreams ☐ Bad Dreams ☐ I don't Remember

Notes :

GOOD HABITS TRACKING :

think POSITIVE

- Cups Of Water I Drank Today : ....
- Exercises : .... Time : ....

☐ Meditation ☐ Reading ☐ Take Vitamins ☐ No Sugar

☐ Eat Healthy ☐ Drink More Water ☐ Socialize

☐ Be Positive ☐ Pray ☐ Family Time ☐ Sleep Early

MOOD TRACKING :

Happy	Sad	Anxious	Lazy	Sick	Flirty	Inlove	Angry
☐	☐	☐	☐	☐	☐	☐	☐

Notes :

PROMPTS

I love life because…

MANIFESTATION

Date : / /

Today I Want To Manifest :

Today I'm Grateful For :

Visualization :

I am...	
I feel...	
I have...	

My Daily Affirmations :

1.	
2.	
3.	

Actions To Take :

1.

2.

3.

TRACKING & REFLECTION

Slept From :....... To : ......

☐ Good Dreams ☐ Bad Dreams ☐ I don't Remember

Notes :

GOOD HABITS TRACKING :

think POSITIVE

- Cups Of Water I Drank Today : ....
- Exercises : .... Time : ....

☐ Meditation ☐ Reading ☐ Take Vitamins ☐ No Sugar

☐ Eat Healthy ☐ Drink More Water ☐ Socialize

☐ Be Positive ☐ Pray ☐ Family Time ☐ Sleep Early

MOOD TRACKING :

Happy	Sad	Anxious	Lazy	Sick	Flirty	Inlove	Angry
☐	☐	☐	☐	☐	☐	☐	☐

Notes :

PROMPTS

Write a thank you letter to yourself.

MANIFESTATION

Date: / /

Today I Want To Manifest:

Today I'm Grateful For:

Visualization:

I am...	
I feel...	
I have...	

My Daily Affirmations:

1.	
2.	
3.	

Actions To Take:

1.
2.
3.

TRACKING & REFLECTION

Slept From :....... To : ......

☐ Good Dreams ☐ Bad Dreams ☐ I don't Remember

Notes :

GOOD HABITS TRACKING :

think POSITIVE

- Cups Of Water I Drank Today : ....
- Exercises : .... Time : ....

☐ Meditation ☐ Reading ☐ Take Vitamins ☐ No Sugar

☐ Eat Healthy ☐ Drink More Water ☐ Socialize

☐ Be Positive ☐ Pray ☐ Family Time ☐ Sleep Early

MOOD TRACKING :

Happy	Sad	Anxious	Lazy	Sick	Flirty	Inlove	Angry
☐	☐	☐	☐	☐	☐	☐	☐

Notes :

PROMPTS

Write a thank you letter to the universe.

MANIFESTATION

Date: / /

Today I Want To Manifest:

Today I'm Grateful For:

Visualization:

I am...	
I feel...	
I have...	

My Daily Affirmations:

1.	
2.	
3.	

Actions To Take:

1. ______
2. ______
3. ______

TRACKING & REFLECTION

Slept From :....... To : ......

☐ Good Dreams ☐ Bad Dreams ☐ I don't Remember

Notes :

GOOD HABITS TRACKING :

think POSITIVE

- Cups Of Water I Drank Today : ....
- Exercises : .... Time : ....

☐ Meditation ☐ Reading ☐ Take Vitamins ☐ No Sugar

☐ Eat Healthy ☐ Drink More Water ☐ Socialize

☐ Be Positive ☐ Pray ☐ Family Time ☐ Sleep Early

MOOD TRACKING :

Happy	Sad	Anxious	Lazy	Sick	Flirty	Inlove	Angry
☐	☐	☐	☐	☐	☐	☐	☐

Notes :

PROMPTS

If you had $10 million dollars in the bank right now, who would you be and what would you do?

MANIFESTATION

Date: / /

Today I Want To Manifest:

Today I'm Grateful For:

Visualization:

I am...	
I feel...	
I have...	

My Daily Affirmations:

1.	
2.	
3.	

Actions To Take:

1.

2.

3.

TRACKING & REFLECTION

Slept From :....... To : ......

☐ Good Dreams ☐ Bad Dreams ☐ I don't Remember

Notes :

GOOD HABITS TRACKING :

think POSITIVE

- Cups Of Water I Drank Today : ....
- Exercises : .... Time : ....

☐ Meditation ☐ Reading ☐ Take Vitamins ☐ No Sugar

☐ Eat Healthy ☐ Drink More Water ☐ Socialize

☐ Be Positive ☐ Pray ☐ Family Time ☐ Sleep Early

MOOD TRACKING :

Happy	Sad	Anxious	Lazy	Sick	Flirty	Inlove	Angry
☐	☐	☐	☐	☐	☐	☐	☐

Notes :

PROMPTS

How much money do you want to earn?

MANIFESTATION

Date: / /

Today I Want To Manifest:

Today I'm Grateful For:

Visualization:

I am...	
I feel...	
I have...	

My Daily Affirmations:

1.	
2.	
3.	

Actions To Take:

1.

2.

3.

TRACKING & REFLECTION

Slept From :....... To : ......

☐ Good Dreams ☐ Bad Dreams ☐ I don't Remember

Notes :

GOOD HABITS TRACKING :

think POSITIVE

- Cups Of Water I Drank Today : ....
- Exercises : .... Time : ....

☐ Meditation ☐ Reading ☐ Take Vitamins ☐ No Sugar

☐ Eat Healthy ☐ Drink More Water ☐ Socialize

☐ Be Positive ☐ Pray ☐ Family Time ☐ Sleep Early

MOOD TRACKING :

Happy	Sad	Anxious	Lazy	Sick	Flirty	Inlove	Angry
☐	☐	☐	☐	☐	☐	☐	☐

Notes :

PROMPTS

What habits/ hobbies make me happy?

MANIFESTATION

Date: / /

Today I Want To Manifest:

Today I'm Grateful For:

Visualization:

I am...	
I feel...	
I have...	

My Daily Affirmations:

1.	
2.	
3.	

Actions To Take:

1.

2.

3.

TRACKING & REFLECTION

Slept From :....... To : ......

☐ Good Dreams ☐ Bad Dreams ☐ I don't Remember

Notes :

GOOD HABITS TRACKING :

think POSITIVE

- Cups Of Water I Drank Today : ....
- Exercises : .... Time : ....

☐ Meditation ☐ Reading ☐ Take Vitamins ☐ No Sugar

☐ Eat Healthy ☐ Drink More Water ☐ Socialize

☐ Be Positive ☐ Pray ☐ Family Time ☐ Sleep Early

MOOD TRACKING :

Happy	Sad	Anxious	Lazy	Sick	Flirty	Inlove	Angry
☐	☐	☐	☐	☐	☐	☐	☐

Notes :

Your Daily Dose Of Affirmations :

I am intelligent

I am strong

I am happy

I am blessed

I am compassion

I am a great person

I am a positive person

I define my individuality

I have decided to stick with love

I accept joy

I accept abundance

I accept honesty

I accept a healthy relationship with everyone

I accept a healthy body

I accept a healthy mind

I accept myself for who I am

PROMPTS

List some of your biggest priorities in life?

MANIFESTATION

Date : / /

Today I Want To Manifest :

Today I'm Grateful For :

Visualization :

I am...	
I feel...	
I have...	

My Daily Affirmations :

1.	
2.	
3.	

Actions To Take :

1.
2.
3.

TRACKING & REFLECTION

Slept From :....... To : ......

☐ Good Dreams ☐ Bad Dreams ☐ I don't Remember

Notes :

GOOD HABITS TRACKING :

think POSITIVE

- Cups Of Water I Drank Today : ....
- Exercises : .... Time : ....

☐ Meditation ☐ Reading ☐ Take Vitamins ☐ No Sugar

☐ Eat Healthy ☐ Drink More Water ☐ Socialize

☐ Be Positive ☐ Pray ☐ Family Time ☐ Sleep Early

MOOD TRACKING :

Happy	Sad	Anxious	Lazy	Sick	Flirty	Inlove	Angry
☐	☐	☐	☐	☐	☐	☐	☐

Notes :

PROMPTS

What are you the most grateful for in your life?

MANIFESTATION

Date: / /

Today I Want To Manifest:

Today I'm Grateful For:

Visualization:

I am...	
I feel...	
I have...	

My Daily Affirmations:

1.	
2.	
3.	

Actions To Take:

1.

2.

3.

TRACKING & REFLECTION

Slept From :....... To : ......

☐ Good Dreams ☐ Bad Dreams ☐ I don't Remember

Notes :

GOOD HABITS TRACKING :

think POSITIVE

- Cups Of Water I Drank Today : ....
- Exercises : .... Time : ....

☐ Meditation ☐ Reading ☐ Take Vitamins ☐ No Sugar

☐ Eat Healthy ☐ Drink More Water ☐ Socialize

☐ Be Positive ☐ Pray ☐ Family Time ☐ Sleep Early

MOOD TRACKING :

Happy	Sad	Anxious	Lazy	Sick	Flirty	Inlove	Angry
☐	☐	☐	☐	☐	☐	☐	☐

Notes :

PROMPTS

What are some amazing things you have already accomplished?

MANIFESTATION

Date : / /

Today I Want To Manifest :

Today I'm Grateful For :

Visualization :

I am...	
I feel...	
I have...	

My Daily Affirmations :

1.	
2.	
3.	

Actions To Take :

1.

2.

3.

TRACKING & REFLECTION

Slept From :....... To : ......

☐ Good Dreams ☐ Bad Dreams ☐ I don't Remember

Notes :

GOOD HABITS TRACKING :

think POSITIVE

- Cups Of Water I Drank Today : ....
- Exercises : .... Time : ....

☐ Meditation ☐ Reading ☐ Take Vitamins ☐ No Sugar

☐ Eat Healthy ☐ Drink More Water ☐ Socialize

☐ Be Positive ☐ Pray ☐ Family Time ☐ Sleep Early

MOOD TRACKING :

Happy	Sad	Anxious	Lazy	Sick	Flirty	Inlove	Angry
☐	☐	☐	☐	☐	☐	☐	☐

Notes :

PROMPTS

Spend a few minutes visualizing your IDEAL life, then write about what you experienced.

MANIFESTATION

Date : / /

Today I Want To Manifest :

Today I'm Grateful For :

Visualization :

I am...	
I feel...	
I have...	

My Daily Affirmations :

1.	
2.	
3.	

Actions To Take :

1.

2.

3.

TRACKING & REFLECTION

Slept From :....... To : ......

☐ Good Dreams ☐ Bad Dreams ☐ I don't Remember

Notes :

GOOD HABITS TRACKING :

think POSITIVE

- Cups Of Water I Drank Today : ....
- Exercises : .... Time : ....

☐ Meditation ☐ Reading ☐ Take Vitamins ☐ No Sugar

☐ Eat Healthy ☐ Drink More Water ☐ Socialize

☐ Be Positive ☐ Pray ☐ Family Time ☐ Sleep Early

MOOD TRACKING :

Happy	Sad	Anxious	Lazy	Sick	Flirty	Inlove	Angry
☐	☐	☐	☐	☐	☐	☐	☐

Notes :

PROMPTS

How do you feel about your physical health right now?

MANIFESTATION

Date : / /

Today I Want To Manifest :

Today I'm Grateful For :

Visualization :

I am...	
I feel...	
I have...	

My Daily Affirmations :

1.	
2.	
3.	

Actions To Take :

1.
2.
3.

TRACKING & REFLECTION

Slept From :....... To : ......

☐ Good Dreams ☐ Bad Dreams ☐ I don't Remember

Notes :

GOOD HABITS TRACKING :

think POSITIVE

- Cups Of Water I Drank Today : ....
- Exercises : .... Time : ....

☐ Meditation ☐ Reading ☐ Take Vitamins ☐ No Sugar

☐ Eat Healthy ☐ Drink More Water ☐ Socialize

☐ Be Positive ☐ Pray ☐ Family Time ☐ Sleep Early

MOOD TRACKING :

Happy	Sad	Anxious	Lazy	Sick	Flirty	Inlove	Angry
☐	☐	☐	☐	☐	☐	☐	☐

Notes :

PROMPTS

How do you feel about your mental health right now?

MANIFESTATION

Date: / /

Today I Want To Manifest:

Today I'm Grateful For:

Visualization:

I am...	
I feel...	
I have...	

My Daily Affirmations:

1.	
2.	
3.	

Actions To Take:

1. ______
2. ______
3. ______

TRACKING & REFLECTION

Slept From :....... To : ......

☐ Good Dreams ☐ Bad Dreams ☐ I don't Remember

Notes :

GOOD HABITS TRACKING :

think POSITIVE

- Cups Of Water I Drank Today : ....
- Exercises : .... Time : ....

☐ Meditation ☐ Reading ☐ Take Vitamins ☐ No Sugar

☐ Eat Healthy ☐ Drink More Water ☐ Socialize

☐ Be Positive ☐ Pray ☐ Family Time ☐ Sleep Early

MOOD TRACKING :

Happy	Sad	Anxious	Lazy	Sick	Flirty	Inlove	Angry
☐	☐	☐	☐	☐	☐	☐	☐

Notes :

PROMPTS

Write down a script of how you wish your day would have gone.

MANIFESTATION

Date : / /

Today I Want To Manifest :

Today I'm Grateful For :

Visualization :

I am...	
I feel...	
I have...	

My Daily Affirmations :

1.	
2.	
3.	

Actions To Take :

1. __________

2. __________

3. __________

TRACKING & REFLECTION

Slept From :....... To : ......

☐ Good Dreams ☐ Bad Dreams ☐ I don't Remember

Notes :

GOOD HABITS TRACKING :

think POSITIVE

- Cups Of Water I Drank Today : ....
- Exercises : .... Time : ....

☐ Meditation ☐ Reading ☐ Take Vitamins ☐ No Sugar

☐ Eat Healthy ☐ Drink More Water ☐ Socialize

☐ Be Positive ☐ Pray ☐ Family Time ☐ Sleep Early

MOOD TRACKING :

Happy	Sad	Anxious	Lazy	Sick	Flirty	Inlove	Angry
☐	☐	☐	☐	☐	☐	☐	☐

Notes :

PROMPTS

What is your deepest, most burning desire right at this moment?

MANIFESTATION

Date: / /

Today I Want To Manifest:

Today I'm Grateful For:

Visualization:

I am...	
I feel...	
I have...	

My Daily Affirmations:

1.	
2.	
3.	

Actions To Take:

1.

2.

3.

TRACKING & REFLECTION

Slept From :....... To : ......

☐ Good Dreams ☐ Bad Dreams ☐ I don't Remember

Notes :

GOOD HABITS TRACKING :

think POSITIVE

- Cups Of Water I Drank Today : ....
- Exercises : .... Time : ....

☐ Meditation ☐ Reading ☐ Take Vitamins ☐ No Sugar

☐ Eat Healthy ☐ Drink More Water ☐ Socialize

☐ Be Positive ☐ Pray ☐ Family Time ☐ Sleep Early

MOOD TRACKING :

Happy	Sad	Anxious	Lazy	Sick	Flirty	Inlove	Angry
☐	☐	☐	☐	☐	☐	☐	☐

Notes :

Your Daily Dose Of Affirmations :

I deserve to be loved

I am beautiful

My black skin is beautiful

People are fond of my skin

People are attracted to me instantly

My skin glows

Every part of me is beautiful

I am comfortable with my own skin

I have a strong willpower

I am proud of myself

I am proud of my culture

I am proud of my upbringing

People around me are supportive

People around me encourage me

PROMPTS

Describe your ideal romantic relationship in vivid detail.

MANIFESTATION

Date : / /

Today I Want To Manifest :

Today I'm Grateful For :

Visualization :

I am...	
I feel...	
I have...	

My Daily Affirmations :

1.	
2.	
3.	

Actions To Take :

1. ____

2. ____

3. ____

TRACKING & REFLECTION

Slept From :....... To : ......

☐ Good Dreams ☐ Bad Dreams ☐ I don't Remember

Notes :

GOOD HABITS TRACKING :

think POSITIVE

- Cups Of Water I Drank Today : ....
- Exercises : .... Time : ....

☐ Meditation ☐ Reading ☐ Take Vitamins ☐ No Sugar

☐ Eat Healthy ☐ Drink More Water ☐ Socialize

☐ Be Positive ☐ Pray ☐ Family Time ☐ Sleep Early

MOOD TRACKING :

Happy	Sad	Anxious	Lazy	Sick	Flirty	Inlove	Angry
☐	☐	☐	☐	☐	☐	☐	☐

Notes :

PROMPTS

How am I bettering myself?

MANIFESTATION

Date : / /

Today I Want To Manifest :

Today I'm Grateful For :

Visualization :

I am...	
I feel...	
I have...	

My Daily Affirmations :

1.	
2.	
3.	

Actions To Take :

1.

2.

3.

TRACKING & REFLECTION

Slept From :....... To : ......

☐ Good Dreams ☐ Bad Dreams ☐ I don't Remember

Notes :

GOOD HABITS TRACKING :

think POSITIVE

- Cups Of Water I Drank Today : ....
- Exercises : .... Time : ....

☐ Meditation ☐ Reading ☐ Take Vitamins ☐ No Sugar

☐ Eat Healthy ☐ Drink More Water ☐ Socialize

☐ Be Positive ☐ Pray ☐ Family Time ☐ Sleep Early

MOOD TRACKING :

Happy	Sad	Anxious	Lazy	Sick	Flirty	Inlove	Angry
☐	☐	☐	☐	☐	☐	☐	☐

Notes :

PROMPTS

What excuses are holding you back?

MANIFESTATION

Date: / /

Today I Want To Manifest:

Today I'm Grateful For:

Visualization:

I am...	
I feel...	
I have...	

My Daily Affirmations:

1.	
2.	
3.	

Actions To Take:

1.

2.

3.

TRACKING & REFLECTION

Slept From :....... To : ......

☐ Good Dreams ☐ Bad Dreams ☐ I don't Remember

Notes :

GOOD HABITS TRACKING :

think POSITIVE

- Cups Of Water I Drank Today : ....
- Exercises : .... Time : ....

☐ Meditation ☐ Reading ☐ Take Vitamins ☐ No Sugar

☐ Eat Healthy ☐ Drink More Water ☐ Socialize

☐ Be Positive ☐ Pray ☐ Family Time ☐ Sleep Early

MOOD TRACKING :

Happy	Sad	Anxious	Lazy	Sick	Flirty	Inlove	Angry
☐	☐	☐	☐	☐	☐	☐	☐

Notes :

PROMPTS

What does your ideal daily routine look like?

MANIFESTATION

Date : / /

Today I Want To Manifest :

Today I'm Grateful For :

Visualization :

I am...	
I feel...	
I have...	

My Daily Affirmations :

1.	
2.	
3.	

Actions To Take :

1.

2.

3.

TRACKING & REFLECTION

Slept From :....... To : ......

☐ Good Dreams ☐ Bad Dreams ☐ I don't Remember

Notes :

GOOD HABITS TRACKING :

think POSITIVE

- Cups Of Water I Drank Today : ....
- Exercises : .... Time : ....

☐ Meditation ☐ Reading ☐ Take Vitamins ☐ No Sugar

☐ Eat Healthy ☐ Drink More Water ☐ Socialize

☐ Be Positive ☐ Pray ☐ Family Time ☐ Sleep Early

MOOD TRACKING :

Happy	Sad	Anxious	Lazy	Sick	Flirty	Inlove	Angry
☐	☐	☐	☐	☐	☐	☐	☐

Notes :

PROMPTS

Write out what your dream job looks like and feels like

MANIFESTATION

Date: / /

Today I Want To Manifest:

Today I'm Grateful For:

Visualization:

I am...	
I feel...	
I have...	

My Daily Affirmations:

1.	
2.	
3.	

Actions To Take:

1.
2.
3.

TRACKING & REFLECTION

Slept From :....... To : ......

☐ Good Dreams ☐ Bad Dreams ☐ I don't Remember

Notes :

GOOD HABITS TRACKING :

think POSITIVE

- Cups Of Water I Drank Today : ....
- Exercises : .... Time : ....

☐ Meditation ☐ Reading ☐ Take Vitamins ☐ No Sugar

☐ Eat Healthy ☐ Drink More Water ☐ Socialize

☐ Be Positive ☐ Pray ☐ Family Time ☐ Sleep Early

MOOD TRACKING :

Happy	Sad	Anxious	Lazy	Sick	Flirty	Inlove	Angry
☐	☐	☐	☐	☐	☐	☐	☐

Notes :

PROMPTS

What are the toxic habits you need to change?

MANIFESTATION

Date: / /

Today I Want To Manifest:

Today I'm Grateful For:

Visualization:

I am...	
I feel...	
I have...	

My Daily Affirmations:

1.	
2.	
3.	

Actions To Take:

1.

2.

3.

TRACKING & REFLECTION

Slept From :....... To : ......

☐ Good Dreams ☐ Bad Dreams ☐ I don't Remember

Notes :

GOOD HABITS TRACKING :

think POSITIVE

- Cups Of Water I Drank Today : ....
- Exercises : .... Time : ....

☐ Meditation ☐ Reading ☐ Take Vitamins ☐ No Sugar

☐ Eat Healthy ☐ Drink More Water ☐ Socialize

☐ Be Positive ☐ Pray ☐ Family Time ☐ Sleep Early

MOOD TRACKING :

Happy	Sad	Anxious	Lazy	Sick	Flirty	Inlove	Angry
☐	☐	☐	☐	☐	☐	☐	☐

Notes :

PROMPTS

Write out exactly what your dream home looks like

MANIFESTATION

Date: / /

Today I Want To Manifest:

Today I'm Grateful For:

Visualization:

I am...	
I feel...	
I have...	

My Daily Affirmations:

1.	
2.	
3.	

Actions To Take:

1.
2.
3.

TRACKING & REFLECTION

Slept From :....... To : ......

☐ Good Dreams ☐ Bad Dreams ☐ I don't Remember

Notes :

GOOD HABITS TRACKING :

think POSITIVE

- Cups Of Water I Drank
  Today : ....
- Exercises : .... Time : ....

☐ Meditation ☐ Reading ☐ Take Vitamins ☐ No Sugar

☐ Eat Healthy ☐ Drink More Water ☐ Socialize

☐ Be Positive ☐ Pray ☐ Family Time ☐ Sleep Early

MOOD TRACKING :

Happy	Sad	Anxious	Lazy	Sick	Flirty	Inlove	Angry
☐	☐	☐	☐	☐	☐	☐	☐

Notes :

PROMPTS

If you could travel anywhere in the world where would it be and why?

MANIFESTATION

Date : / /

Today I Want To Manifest :

Today I'm Grateful For :

Visualization :

I am...	
I feel...	
I have...	

My Daily Affirmations :

1.	
2.	
3.	

Actions To Take :

1.

2.

3.

TRACKING & REFLECTION

Slept From :....... To : ......

☐ Good Dreams ☐ Bad Dreams ☐ I don't Remember

Notes :

GOOD HABITS TRACKING :

think POSITIVE

- Cups Of Water I Drank Today : ....
- Exercises : .... Time : ....

☐ Meditation ☐ Reading ☐ Take Vitamins ☐ No Sugar

☐ Eat Healthy ☐ Drink More Water ☐ Socialize

☐ Be Positive ☐ Pray ☐ Family Time ☐ Sleep Early

MOOD TRACKING :

Happy	Sad	Anxious	Lazy	Sick	Flirty	Inlove	Angry
☐	☐	☐	☐	☐	☐	☐	☐

Notes :

PROMPTS

If you had any super power, what would it be and why?

MANIFESTATION

Date: / /

Today I Want To Manifest:

Today I'm Grateful For:

Visualization:

I am...	
I feel...	
I have...	

My Daily Affirmations:

1.	
2.	
3.	

Actions To Take:

1. ______

2. ______

3. ______

TRACKING & REFLECTION

Slept From :....... To : ......

☐ Good Dreams ☐ Bad Dreams ☐ I don't Remember

Notes :

GOOD HABITS TRACKING :

think POSITIVE

- Cups Of Water I Drank Today : ....
- Exercises : .... Time : ....

☐ Meditation ☐ Reading ☐ Take Vitamins ☐ No Sugar

☐ Eat Healthy ☐ Drink More Water ☐ Socialize

☐ Be Positive ☐ Pray ☐ Family Time ☐ Sleep Early

MOOD TRACKING :

Happy	Sad	Anxious	Lazy	Sick	Flirty	Inlove	Angry
☐	☐	☐	☐	☐	☐	☐	☐

Notes :

PROMPTS

If someone asked you to describe yourself, what would you say?

MANIFESTATION

Date : / /

Today I Want To Manifest :

Today I'm Grateful For :

Visualization :

I am...	
I feel...	
I have...	

My Daily Affirmations :

1.	
2.	
3.	

Actions To Take :

1. ______

2. ______

3. ______

TRACKING & REFLECTION

Slept From :....... To : ......

☐ Good Dreams ☐ Bad Dreams ☐ I don't Remember

Notes :

GOOD HABITS TRACKING :

think POSITIVE

- Cups Of Water I Drank Today : ....
- Exercises : .... Time : ....

☐ Meditation ☐ Reading ☐ Take Vitamins ☐ No Sugar

☐ Eat Healthy ☐ Drink More Water ☐ Socialize

☐ Be Positive ☐ Pray ☐ Family Time ☐ Sleep Early

MOOD TRACKING :

Happy	Sad	Anxious	Lazy	Sick	Flirty	Inlove	Angry
☐	☐	☐	☐	☐	☐	☐	☐

Notes :

PROMPTS

If you could describe your life in one word, what would it be and why?

MANIFESTATION

Date: / /

Today I Want To Manifest:

Today I'm Grateful For:

Visualization:

I am...	
I feel...	
I have...	

My Daily Affirmations:

1.	
2.	
3.	

Actions To Take:

1.

2.

3.

TRACKING & REFLECTION

Slept From :....... To : ......

☐ Good Dreams ☐ Bad Dreams ☐ I don't Remember

Notes :

GOOD HABITS TRACKING :

think POSITIVE

- Cups Of Water I Drank Today : ....
- Exercises : .... Time : ....

☐ Meditation ☐ Reading ☐ Take Vitamins ☐ No Sugar

☐ Eat Healthy ☐ Drink More Water ☐ Socialize

☐ Be Positive ☐ Pray ☐ Family Time ☐ Sleep Early

MOOD TRACKING :

Happy	Sad	Anxious	Lazy	Sick	Flirty	Inlove	Angry
☐	☐	☐	☐	☐	☐	☐	☐

Notes :

Your Daily Dose Of Affirmations :

I am filled with joy

I am filled with happiness

I give and receive love

I am the hero of my own story

I work hard to achieve my goal

I am a good person

I believe in myself

I am filled with love for myself

My body is a gift and I love it

My mistakes are stepping stones for success

I am worth everything I desire

I have everything that I desire

I am worthy of love

People love me for who I am

Everybody respects me

Everyone loves me

PROMPTS

What advice would you give to your younger self regarding money?

MANIFESTATION

Date: / /

Today I Want To Manifest:

Today I'm Grateful For:

Visualization:

I am...	
I feel...	
I have...	

My Daily Affirmations:

1.	
2.	
3.	

Actions To Take:

1.

2.

3.

TRACKING & REFLECTION

Slept From :....... To : ......

☐ Good Dreams ☐ Bad Dreams ☐ I don't Remember

Notes :

GOOD HABITS TRACKING :

think POSITIVE

- Cups Of Water I Drank Today : ....
- Exercises : .... Time : ....

☐ Meditation ☐ Reading ☐ Take Vitamins ☐ No Sugar

☐ Eat Healthy ☐ Drink More Water ☐ Socialize

☐ Be Positive ☐ Pray ☐ Family Time ☐ Sleep Early

MOOD TRACKING :

Happy	Sad	Anxious	Lazy	Sick	Flirty	Inlove	Angry
☐	☐	☐	☐	☐	☐	☐	☐

Notes :

PROMPTS

What does it mean to have an abundant life?

MANIFESTATION

Date : / /

Today I Want To Manifest :

Today I'm Grateful For :

Visualization :

I am...	
I feel...	
I have...	

My Daily Affirmations :

1.	
2.	
3.	

Actions To Take :

1.

2.

3.

TRACKING & REFLECTION

Slept From :....... To : ......

☐ Good Dreams ☐ Bad Dreams ☐ I don't Remember

Notes :

GOOD HABITS TRACKING :

think POSITIVE

- Cups Of Water I Drank Today : ....
- Exercises : .... Time : ....

☐ Meditation ☐ Reading ☐ Take Vitamins ☐ No Sugar

☐ Eat Healthy ☐ Drink More Water ☐ Socialize

☐ Be Positive ☐ Pray ☐ Family Time ☐ Sleep Early

MOOD TRACKING :

Happy	Sad	Anxious	Lazy	Sick	Flirty	Inlove	Angry
☐	☐	☐	☐	☐	☐	☐	☐

Notes :

PROMPTS

Month in Review: What lessons did you learn this month?

Made in the USA
Middletown, DE
18 April 2025

74508363R00075